# United States Coins

## Written by Bonita Ferraro

Celebration Press

*Parsippany, New Jersey*

# Yesterday's Coins

People in the United States have
been using coins for hundreds
of years. We use them to buy all
kinds of goods and services, just
as people did in the 1600s. But
the coins we use today are very
different from those used by the
earliest Americans.

**Spanish Milled
Dollar**

In the 1600s, early American
settlers used coins made in European
countries. One popular silver coin was from
Spain. It was called a Spanish Milled Dollar
and was worth 8 reales (ray AHL ays). This
coin was often chopped into eight equal "bits."
It was used as a dollar in the United States for
over a hundred years. Have you ever heard a
quarter called two bits? Now you know why!

Tree coins were some of the earliest coins made in America. They had an oak tree, a pine tree, or a willow tree on them. Making them took a long time. The images were pounded into strips of metal and then cut out with shears, one at a time. The edges of these handmade coins often had to be trimmed to make them all the same weight. Sometimes, dishonest people saved the trimmings and then melted them down to make new coins!

Pine Tree Coin

First United States Coin

The first coin of the new country of the United States of America was a copper penny. It had the words "We Are One" in the middle of 13 joined circles. There was one circle for each of the 13 colonies. The other side said, "Mind Your Business!"

Many early United States coins showed a
woman's head. The woman was called Liberty.
She was a reminder that people came to this
country in search of freedom.

Half Dime

**Indian Head Penny**

Native Americans were honored on two early U.S. coins. It is not certain who the model was for the Indian princess on this penny. Some say that it was Sarah Longacre, the daughter of James Longacre, who designed this coin in 1859.

The model for the buffalo on the Buffalo nickel came from New York's Central Park Zoo. The buffalo's name was Black Diamond. The Indian on the other side of the nickel was modeled after three Indian chiefs: Big Tree, Iron Tail, and Two Moons. This coin honored both American Indians and the buffalo that were so important to their way of life.

Buffalo Nickel

Lincoln Penny
(1909–1959)

Lincoln Penny
(after 1959)

## Today's Coins

The Lincoln penny first appeared in 1909. One side shows Abraham Lincoln. Until 1959 this penny had wheat ears on the other side. Now the other side shows the Lincoln Memorial in Washington, D.C. Look hard and maybe you can find some of the old ones!

In the 1930s the government held a contest to find a design for the Thomas Jefferson nickel. About 400 artists tried for the $1,000 prize money. An artist named Felix Schlag won. His nickel, which had a profile of Thomas Jefferson on one side and Jefferson's home, Monticello, on the other, was first minted in 1938.

Jefferson Nickel

Roosevelt Dime

The dime we use today honors Franklin D. Roosevelt, who was president from 1933 to 1945. He helped the United States through some very hard times, including the Great Depression and World War II. His face first appeared on the dime in 1946. Roosevelt died in office in 1945, the only president ever to be elected four times.

Today's quarters have George Washington's face on one side. Until 1999, quarters always had an eagle on the other side. But starting in 1999, 50 new quarters are being designed, one for each state. By 2009 there will be quarters honoring all 50 states. Many coin collectors will be on the lookout for all 50.

Washington Quarters

**Kennedy Half Dollar**

The Kennedy half dollar is the latest coin to show a U.S. president. It was first made in 1964 to honor President John F. Kennedy, who had died the year before. The first version of this coin showed the presidential seal on the reverse side. The coin now shows Independence Hall in Philadelphia.

The newest U.S. coin honors Sacagawea (sak uh juh WEE uh). This American Indian woman helped lead explorers Lewis and Clark through the northwest part of the United States in the early 1800s. The dollar coin is gold in color, but it's really made of copper, brass, and other metals. Its edge is wide and smooth, so it both looks and feels different from a quarter. This coin replaces the Susan B. Anthony dollar, which never became popular because it was too much like a quarter.

Sacagawea Dollar

Susan B. Anthony Dollar

# Time Line of United States Coins

## 1600s

## 1700s

Spanish Milled Dollar
Early 1600s

First National Coin
1787

Pine Tree Coin 1652

Liberty Half Dime
1792

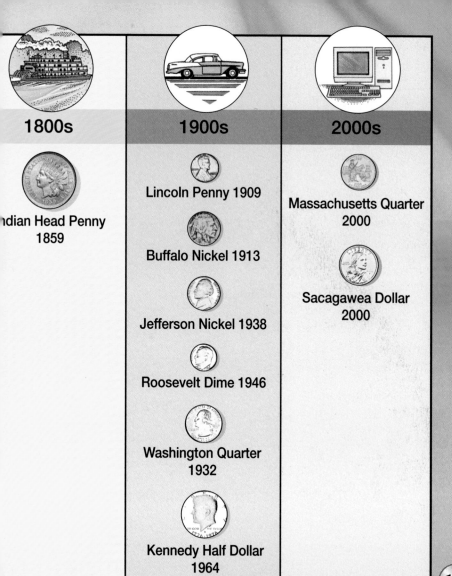

## 1800s

Indian Head Penny
1859

## 1900s

Lincoln Penny 1909

Buffalo Nickel 1913

Jefferson Nickel 1938

Roosevelt Dime 1946

Washington Quarter
1932

Kennedy Half Dollar
1964

## 2000s

Massachusetts Quarter
2000

Sacagawea Dollar
2000

## Did You Know?

¢ A place where coins are made is called a mint.

¢ The mint in Denver, Colorado, makes 1 million coins an hour.

¢ Worn-out coins are melted down and made into new coins.